_____

Your Name Here

TABLE OF CONTENTS

1   PERSONAL INFORMATION
         Your personal information

2, 3   MEDICAL HISTORY @ A GLANCE
         Your personal information

4, 5, 6   MEDICATION
         List all of your medications and the pharmacy of your choice

7   SURGICAL HISTORY
         List all surgeries and schedule surgeries

8, 9   PHYSICIANS LIST
         List all doctor appointments and insurance

10   IMMUNIZATIONS & INSURANCE INFORMATION
         List all of your immunizations/shots and insurance information

11   BLOOD PRESSURE LOG
         List your blood pressure and pulse

12   BLOOD SUGAR LOG
         List your blood sugar at different times of day

13   INSULIN INTAKE
         Keep track of your daily insulin intake

14   EJECTION FRACTION
         List your heart pumping ability

15, 16   RESUSCITATION
         Date of decision with your signature

17, 18   QUALITY OF LIFE INSTRUCTIONS
         Make your medical choices while you are able body and mind

19   APPOINTMENTS
         Keep track of upcoming appointments

20   TRAVEL LOG
         Keep track of all your travel receipts

21   SELF CARE GOALS
         Write down your goals for good health

MY MEDICAL RECORDS @ A GLANCE INTRODUCTION

My Medical Records @ A Glance is a booklet that was created to help make life a little easier and give some structure to the unorganized way we take care of our health. When visiting the doctor's office or health care facilities, we always have to complete certain types of paper work or forms. So many of us are unprepared and unorganized when it comes to gathering the information we need to complete the forms, for example, (looking through wallets, purses, cell phones for insurance cards, phone numbers, etc.). If you could have all of your medical information in one place, wouldn't that be great! That is exactly what My Medical Records @ A Glance booklet will do for you. All of the medical information you need when visiting the doctor's office is in this booklet. Just fill out the forms once and keep them forever; make copies and give to your family members or your caregiver. This booklet is a great tool for getting organized and keeping all of your medical information up to date while building your own medical history.

Nine out of ten people cannot remember what medications they take on a daily basis. Here are a few benefits of having this booklet: the medication list in this booklet will keep track of all your medications; you can add new medicines or delete old ones. This booklet puts all of your information in one place, stores your doctors name and numbers, your immunizations, your last X-Ray, your last mammogram, your last EKG, etc. I could go on and on about the benefits of having this booklet. Maybe you're having your first child. Maybe you just found out you have Cancer, Dementia, Diabetes, or Alzheimer's all of these conditions require good record keeping.

How many people take the time or even have the money to prepare a living will? The Quality of Life Instructions in this booklet can act as a decision maker; just like a living will for medical decisions. The Ejection Fraction Sheet in this booklet is great for keeping track of your heart health. This booklet can be a life-saving tool that helps you monitor your health.

I am a forty-nine year old woman with Focal Segmental Glomerulosclerosis (FSGS) kidney failure; I'm on dialysis and awaiting a kidney transplant. I have to travel to Vanderbilt Hospital in Nashville every so often for appointments and tests, I also have my dialysis, my nephrologist, and my internal medicine doctor visits. I have to keep track of every form, and every little receipt for reimbursement insurance. While keeping up with my own medical information, I discovered an efficient way of organizing the way I monitor my health condition. Having all of my medical information at a glance has proven to be very helpful; so helpful that I put this booklet together to help others organize their own medical information and have it ready and available at a glance.

Sincerely,

Janice Hunter Smith

PERSONAL INFORMATION

NAME _____
       FIRST   LAST   MI

AGE _____ **DATE OF BIRTH** ___ / ___ / ___ **SEX** MALE ☐ FEMALE ☐
                              MONTH   DAY   YEAR

HEIGHT _____ **WEIGHT** _____ **GAIN** _____ **LOSS** _____

DRIVER'S LICENSE # _____ **SSN** ___ - ___ - ___

ADDRESS _____
         STREET   APT #

_____
CITY   STATE   ZIP CODE

DAYTIME PHONE (___) ___ - ___   **CELL PHONE** (___) ___ - ___

EMAIL _____

SPOUSE'S NAME (___) ___ - ___   **PHONE** (___) ___ - ___

ALTERNATE CONTACT _____ **RELATIONSHIP** _____

DAYTIME PHONE (___) ___ - ___   **CELL PHONE** (___) ___ - ___

ALLERGIES _____
_____

BLOOD TYPE
           O   A   B   AB
         +☐ −☐   +☐ −☐   +☐ −☐   +☐ −☐

MEDICAL HISTORY @ A GLANCE

	YES	NO	IF YES, PLEASE EXPLAIN
TBC (TUBERCULOSIS)	☐	☐	
NEURALGIC DISEASE	☐	☐	
HEART DISEASE	☐	☐	
LIVER DISEASE	☐	☐	
LUNG DISEASE	☐	☐	
KIDNEY DISEASE	☐	☐	
DIABETES	☐	☐	
BLEEDING DISORDER	☐	☐	
GI DISEASE (STOMACH)	☐	☐	
ALLERGIES	☐	☐	
DRUGS	☐	☐	
STEROIDS	☐	☐	
DENTURES	☐	☐	
CONTACT LENS	☐	☐	
COUGH	☐	☐	
SMOKE (PACKS PER DAY)	☐	☐	
MOTION SICKNESS	☐	☐	
OTHER	☐	☐	
	☐	☐	
	☐	☐	
	☐	☐	
	☐	☐	

MEDICAL HISTORY @ A GLANCE continued

HAVE YOU EVER HAD A TRANSPLANT OF ANY TYPE? YES ☐ NO ☐
IF YES, EXPLAIN ....

DO YOU HAVE A HISTORY OF CANCER? YES ☐ NO ☐
IF YES, EXPLAIN ....

HAVE YOU HAD CHEMO IN THE LAST 12 MONTHS? YES ☐ NO ☐

RADIATION THERAPY? YES ☐ NO ☐

PREVENTATIVE HEALTH CARE INFORMATION:
(date, year and location of last test)

CHEST X-RAY ....

ELECTROCARDIOGRAM (EKG) ....

MAMMOGRAM ....

CHOLESTEROL ....

COLON EXAM ....

PELVIC/PAP SMEAR ....

SMOKE: # PACKS PER DAY ....

ALCOHOL USAGE ....

MEDICATIONS

MEDICATION	DOSAGE	REASON	PRESCRIBING DOCTOR

PHARMACY ....
ADDRESS ....
PHONE (.........) .... - ....

MEDICATIONS continued

MEDICATION	DOSAGE	REASON	PRESCRIBING DOCTOR

PHARMACY ....

ADDRESS ....

PHONE (..........) .... - ....

MEDICATIONS continued

MEDICATION	DOSAGE	REASON	PRESCRIBING DOCTOR

PHARMACY ....
ADDRESS ....
PHONE (........) .... - ....

SURGICAL HISTORY

SURGERY					DATE		REASON		SURGEON

PHYSICIAN LIST

PHYSICIAN ....

TYPE OF PHYSICIAN ....

PHONE (........) .... - .... **EMAIL** ....

PHYSICIAN ....

TYPE OF PHYSICIAN ....

PHONE (........) .... - .... **EMAIL** ....

PHYSICIAN ....

TYPE OF PHYSICIAN ....

PHONE (........) .... - .... **EMAIL** ....

PHYSICIAN ....

TYPE OF PHYSICIAN ....

PHONE (........) .... - .... **EMAIL** ....

HOSPITAL/MEDICAL CENTER/CLINIC

....

....

....

....

....

....

PHYSICIAN LIST continued

PHYSICIAN ....

TYPE OF PHYSICIAN ....

PHONE (_____) _____ - _____   **EMAIL** ....

PHYSICIAN ....

TYPE OF PHYSICIAN ....

PHONE (_____) _____ - _____   **EMAIL** ....

PHYSICIAN ....

TYPE OF PHYSICIAN ....

PHONE (_____) _____ - _____   **EMAIL** ....

PHYSICIAN ....

TYPE OF PHYSICIAN ....

PHONE (_____) _____ - _____   **EMAIL** ....

HOSPITAL/MEDICAL CENTER/CLINIC

....

....

....

....

....

IMMUNIZATIONS

	YES	NO	DATE
PNEUMOVAX/PNEUMONIA	☐	☐	
TUBERCULOSIS(TB) SKIN TEST	☐	☐	
HEPATITIS B1	☐	☐	
HEPATITIS B2	☐	☐	
HEPATITIS B3	☐	☐	
OTHER	☐	☐	

HAVE YOU HAD:

	YES	NO	DATE
RUBELLA (GERMAN MEASLES)	☐	☐	
RUBEOLA (MEASLES)	☐	☐	
FLU	☐	☐	
HEPATITAS A	☐	☐	
TETANUS	☐	☐	
OTHER	☐	☐	

INSURANCE INFORMATION

PRIMARY INSURANCE _____

ID # _____ GROUP # _____

SECONDARY INSURANCE _____

ID # _____ GROUP # _____

OTHER INSURANCE _____

ID # _____ GROUP # _____

DAILY BLOOD PRESSURE LOG

DATE	MORNING			EVENING		
	TIME	B/P	PULSE	TIME	B/P	PULSE

GOAL:

BLOOD SUGAR LOG

DATE	TIME	READING	DATE	TIME	READING

GOAL:

DAILY INSULIN INTAKE

	DATE	INSULIN NAME	MG/DL OR MMOL/L	BREAKFAST	LUNCH	DINNER	BEDTIME	NOTES
MON								
TUES								
WED								
THURS								
FRI								
SAT								
SUN								
MON								
TUES								
WED								
THURS								
FRI								
SAT								
SUN								
MON								
TUES								
WED								
THURS								
FRI								
SAT								
SUN								

EF – EJECTION FRACTION

Ejection Fraction is the key indicator of your heart's health. EF is the percentage of blood that is pumped from your heart during each beat. You may wish to discuss your EF with your physician. Use this tracker to record your EF number and answer to your questions.

NORMAL	BELOW NORMAL	HIGH RISK
50-75%	36-49%	35%

After finding out what your EF is keep track of it with this chart:

DATE	NORMAL	DATE	BELOW	DATE	HIGH

RESUSCITATION

YES ☐   NO ☐

This Resuscitation Sheet is based on the medical conditions and wishes of the person identified on this form. Any section not completed indicates full treatment for that section. When need occurs, **first** follow these resuscitation instructions, **then** contact physician.

NAME .... DATE OF BIRTH ..../........../..........
                                                                              MONTH   DAY   YEAR

SECTION 1 - CHECK ONE BOX ONLY

CARDIOPULMONARY RESUSCITATION (CPR): Patient has no pulse and/or is not breathing.
- ☐ Resuscitate (CPR)
- ☐ Do Not Attempt Resuscitate (DNR/no CPR)

When not in cardiopulmonary arrest, follow orders in B, C, and D

SECTION 2 - CHECK ONE BOX ONLY

MEDICAL INTERVENTIONS: Patient has pulse and/or is breathing.
- ☐ Comfort Measures. Treat with dignity and respect. Keep clean, warm, and dry. Use medication by any route, positioning, wound care and other measures to relieve pain and suffering. Use oxygen, suction and manual treatment of airway obstruction as needed for comfort. Do not transfer to hospital for life sustaining treatment. Transfer only if comfort needs cannot be met in current location.
- ☐ Limited Additional Interventions, includes care described above. Use medical treatment, IV fluids and cardiac monitoring as indicated. Do not use intubations, advanced airway intervention, or mechanical ventilation. Transfer to hospital if indicated. Avoid intensive care.
- ☐ Full treatment. Includes care above. Use intubation, advanced airway interventions mechanical ventilation, and cardioversion as indicated. Transfer to hospital if indicated.

SECTION 3 - CHECK ONE BOX ONLY

ANTIBIOTICS: Treatment for new medical conditions.
- ☐ No Antibiotics
- ☐ Antibiotics
- ☐ Other Instructions: ....

SECTION 4 - CHECK ONE BOX IN EACH COLUMN

MEDICALLY ADMINISTERED FLUIDS AND NUTRITION: Oral fluids and nutrition must be offered if medically feasible.

- ☐ No IV fluids *(provide other measures to assure comfort)*
- ☐ IV fluids for a defined trial period
- ☐ IV fluids long-term if indicated

- ☐ No feeding tube
- ☐ Feeding tube for defined time period
- ☐ Feeding tube long-term

RESUSCITATION continued

SECTION 5 - ALL MUST BE COMPLETED

DISCUSSED WITH:
- ☐ Patient/Resident
- ☐ Healthcare agent
- ☐ Court-appointed guardian
- ☐ Healthcare surrogate
- ☐ Parent of minor
- ☐ Other: _____

THE BASIS FOR THESE INSTRUCTIONS:
- ☐ Patient's preferences
- ☐ Patient's best interest *(patient lacks capacity or preferences unknown)*
- ☐ Medical indications
- ☐ Other: _____

DOCTOR _____ PHONE (____) ____ - ____

Significant thought has been given to life-sustaining treatment. Preferences have been expressed to a physician and/or health care professional(s). This document reflects those treatment preferences by patient. (If signed by any one other than patient, preferences expressed must reflect patient's wishes as best understood by surrogate).

SIGNATURE _____ PHONE (____) ____ - ____

PRINTED NAME _____

SURROGATE _____ PHONE (____) ____ - ____

RELATIONSHIP _____ DATE ____ / ____ / ____
                                         MONTH   DAY   YEAR

HEALTHCARE PROFESSIONAL PREPARING FORM _____

PREPARE TITLE _____ PHONE (____) ____ - ____

COMPLETING POST: Must be completed by a health care professional based on patient preferences, patient best interest, and medical indications. POST must be signed by a physician to be valid; Verbal orders are acceptable with follow-up signature by physician in accordance with facility/community policy. Photocopies/faxes of signed POST forms are legal and valid.

USING POST: Any incomplete section of POST implies full treatment for that section.
No defibrillator (including AEDs) should be used on a person who has chosen "Do Not Attempt Resuscitation". Oral fluids and nutrition must always be offered if medically feasible. IV medication to enhance comfort may be appropriate for a person who has chosen "Comfort Measures Only". Treatment of dehydration is a measure, which prolongs life. A person who desires IV fluids should indicate "Limited Interventions" or "Full Treatment". A person with capacity, or the surrogate of a person without capacity, can request alternative treatment.

REVIEWING POST: This POST should be reviewed if: The patient is transferred from one care setting or care level to another. There is a substantial change in the patient's health status. The patient's treatment preferences change. Draw line through sections 1 through 5 and write "VOID" in large letters if POST is replaced or becomes invalid.

QUALITY OF LIFE INSTRUCTIONS

Competent adults and emancipated minors may give advance instructions using this form or any form of their own choosing. To be legally binding, the Quality of Life Instruction's Sheet must be signed and either witnessed or notarized.

I, _____, hereby give these advance instructions on how I want to be treated by my doctors and other health care providers when I can no longer make those treatment decisions myself on my own.

I WANT THE FOLLOWING PERSON TO MAKE HEALTH CARE DECISIONS FOR ME:

NAME _____ PHONE (___) ___-_____

RELATIONSHIP _____ DATE ___/___/___
                                  MONTH DAY YEAR

ADDRESS _____

QUALITY OF LIFE

I want my doctors to help me maintain an acceptable quality of life including adequate pain management. A quality of life that is unacceptable to me means when I have any of the following conditions *(you can check as many of these items as you want)*:

- [ ] **Permanent Unconscious Condition:** I become totally unaware of people or surroundings with no chance of ever waking up from the coma after ___ months.
- [ ] **Permanent Confusion:** I become unable to remember, understand or make my own decisions. I do not recognize loved ones and cannot ever again have a clear conversation with them after ___ months.
- [ ] **Dependent in all Activities of Daily Living:** I am no longer able to talk clearly or move by myself. I depend on others for feeding, bathing, dressing and walking. Rehabilitation or any other restorative treatment will not help after ___ months.
- [ ] **End-Stage Illnesses:** I have an illness that has reached its final stages in spite of full treatment. Examples: Widespread cancer that does not respond any more to treatment; chronic and/or damaged heart and lungs, where oxygen needed most of the time and activities have completely stopped due to the feeling of suffocation after ___ months.

TREATMENT

If my quality of life becomes unacceptable to me and my condition is irreversible (it will not improve), I direct that medically appropriate treatment be provided as follows:
Checking "yes" means I WANT the treatment. Checking "no" means I DO NOT want the treatment.

YES NO
- [ ] [ ] **CPR (CARDIOPULMONARY RESUSCITATION):** To make the heart beat again and restore breathing after it has stopped. Usually this involves electric shock, chest compressions, and breathing assistance.
- [ ] [ ] **LIFE SUPPORT/OTHER ARTIFICIAL SUPPORT:** Continuous use of breathing machines, IV fluids, medications, and other equipment that helps the lungs, heart, kidney and other organs to continue to work.
- [ ] [ ] **TREATMENT OF NEW CONDITIONS:** Use of surgery, blood transfusions, or antibiotics that will deal with a new condition but will not help the main illness.
- [ ] [ ] **TUBE FEEDING/IV FLUIDS:** Use of tubes to deliver food and water to patient's stomach or use of IV fluids into a vein which would include artificially delivered nutrition and hydration.

QUALITY OF LIFE INSTRUCTIONS continued

INSTRUCTIONS (SUCH AS HOSPICE CARE, BURIAL ARRANGEMENTS, ETC.):

....
....
....
....

ORGAN DONATION (OPTIONAL)

Upon my death, I wish to make the following anatomical gift (please mark one).
- ☐ Any organ/tissue
- ☐ My entire body
- ☐ Only the following organs/tissues: ....

Your signature should either be witnessed by two competent adults or notarized. If witnessed, neither witness should be the person you appointed as your agent. At least one of the witnesses should be someone who is not related to you or entitled to any part of your estate.

SIGNATURE .... **DATE** .... / .... / ....
                                                                                        MONTH   DAY   YEAR

WITNESSES

WITNESS 1 ....

I am a competent adult who is not named as the agent. I witnessed the patient's signature on this form.

WITNESS 2 ....

I am a competent adult who is not named as the agent. I am not related to the patient by blood, marriage, or adoption and I would not be entitled to any portion of the patient's estate upon his or her death under any existing will or codicil or by operation of law. I witnessed the patient's signature on this form.

* This document may be notarized instead of witnessed.

APPOINTMENTS

DOCTOR	DATE	/ /	TIME	: AM
		MONTH DAY YEAR		PM

INSTRUCTIONS

PHONE ( ) -   LOCATION

DOCTOR	DATE	/ /	TIME	: AM
		MONTH DAY YEAR		PM

INSTRUCTIONS

PHONE ( ) -   LOCATION

DOCTOR	DATE	/ /	TIME	: AM
		MONTH DAY YEAR		PM

INSTRUCTIONS

PHONE ( ) -   LOCATION

DOCTOR	DATE	/ /	TIME	: AM
		MONTH DAY YEAR		PM

INSTRUCTIONS

PHONE ( ) -   LOCATION

DOCTOR	DATE	/ /	TIME	: AM
		MONTH DAY YEAR		PM

INSTRUCTIONS

PHONE ( ) -   LOCATION

DOCTOR	DATE	/ /	TIME	: AM
		MONTH DAY YEAR		PM

INSTRUCTIONS

PHONE ( ) -   LOCATION

DOCTOR	DATE	/ /	TIME	: AM
		MONTH DAY YEAR		PM

INSTRUCTIONS

PHONE ( ) -   LOCATION

TRAVEL LOG

Save all of your receipts and send itemized originals along with this form to your Insurance Company. Keep copies for your records.

CASE MANAGER _____

EMPLOYEE _____ **SSN** ___ - ___ - ___

RECIPIENT _____ **RELATIONSHIP TO EMPLOYEE** _____

COMPANION _____ **RELATIONSHIP TO RECIPIENT** _____

DATES OF TRIP _____ **PURPOSE OF TRIP** _____

ORGAN TYPE _____ **NAME & STATE OF FACILITY** _____

DATE OF TRAVEL	PRIVATE VEHICLE MILES	RENTAL VEHICLE MILES	GASOLINE	HOTEL AND LODGING	MEALS AND TIPS	GROCERIES	AIR/RAIL TRAVEL	PARKING	TAXI/BUS COST

Attach all receipts

MISCELLANEOUS ITEMS _____

_____

_____

_____

RECIPIENT'S SIGNATURE _____ **DATE** ___ / ___ / ___
                                                        MONTH DAY YEAR

SELF CARE GOALS

....
....
....
....
....
....
....
....
....
....
....
....
....
....
....
....
....
....

A MERRY HEART DOES GOOD, LIKE MEDICINE.

PROVERBS 17:22

I KNOW THAT THERE IS NOTHING BETTER FOR MEN AND WOMEN THAN TO BE HAPPY AND DO GOOD WHILE THEY LIVE.

ECCLESIASTES 3:13

IT IS GOOD AND PROPER FOR A MAN TO EAT AND DRINK, AND TO FIND SATISFACTION IN HIS TOILSOME LABOR UNDER THE SUN DURING THE FEW DAYS OF HIS LIFE.

ECCLESIASTES 5:18

A special thanks to my mother and father,
Pastor Willie C. and Peggy Hunter

www.ingramcontent.com/pod-product-compliance
Lightning Source LLC
LaVergne TN
LVHW070541070526
838199LV00076B/6819